INTERNET MARKETING GUIDE

FOR BEGINNERS

By Robert Julius

Table of Contents

Copyright and disclaimer notice

in your marketplace. The author is not part of any legal team. The purpose of this book is to create awareness and educate people on how to start their internet marketing the right way. The author of this book and publisher is not responsible for any omission or error because the book is completed and well researched to the best of his knowledge.

Introduction

There are many books out there today about Internet marketing and how to make money online but to be realistic for you to find a well explained book and latest information about digital marketing is rare. That is why this book is different because it takes me years of research, time, money and energy to put this information together for the usefulness and benefit of the public as a whole. There are a lot of books and manuals about achieving success on Amazon, eBay, affiliate marketing and so on but despite all these available resources 90% of new marketers fail to make money online they also end up losing money online and their aim is to make money online.

That is the main reason this book will be of help to new Internet marketer or aspiring one because the lesson in this book is a guide to their success and a time saving book so that they won't continue wasting money, time and their resources online anymore. All you need is to pay attention we are in the 21st century and it is your time to be successful online and build a business that guarantees you good income daily. Your journey to success start now only by you implementing all the lessons you are about to learn in this Book more so there is no doubt that one can become a successful digital marketer within a short period of time that can be achievable if you have a clear understanding of the basic skills and concept of internet marketing because good foundation matters in any skills you may decide to learn. There are a lot of lessons provided in this book so it is all yours. Relax and concentrate for your better understanding.

Knowledge is power

The term knowledge is the key asset to anything you want to do in life because without knowledge anything will not be achievable besides most copycat would have done things in a very different way if they had a better definition and understanding of what they intend to start. Because having an idea or an opportunity is not a big deal but implementation is the key because turning the opportunity or an idea into a money making machine is a different aspect entirely because idea without proper implementation is meaningless. Because the first thing is to discover yourself that is what are you good at, what idea do you have or skill that you can turn to a profitable business for example you love making cosmetics and skincare products for women you can decided to build your business in this niche you can organise a seminar on how to do it or selling information products on how to do it the right way. If you can do all this this will help you generate the capital to start this business easily without going to meet people to borrow you money to start the business. This is how I started my business too by teaching people the skill i have through seminars, empowerment programs and much more and charge them some money for them to be able to attend the seminar because am giving out value in return of money.

Even mahatma Gandhi of blessed memory says live as if you were to die tomorrow and learn as if you were to live forever.

Building a strong foundation

The most problem new business owner and Internet market have is that they want to start business today and start making a good return immediately but they have forgotten Rome wasn't built in a day and the only way to get started is to build your brand online with good reputation such as good customer service, prompt response to questions, quick delivery and you have to know that customers is always right the reason why all this is very essential is that people are afraid of scams online and you need to convince them you are not a scam so you need to stand out if you can stick to all these idea and principles money will never be your problem again and your business will grow beyond imagination but it requires a lot of time, hard work, years and consistency to achieve this once you have been recognised with all these attribute you will be amaze with a lot of referrals by your previous customers even without you running a sponsor ad you will consistently making money online with ease.

I will advise you to apply all these strategies to your business then you will be amazed when your business starts flourishing online this only happens because of the trust people have in you.

Why people get duped and scam

The reason why a lot of Internet marketers get scammed online is because they lack comprehension because most fresh internet marketers doesn't know what they are doing because at times they are being gullible and this makes them number one target for internet fraudster for example you intend to travel to a country their culture and language is different from yours country like Saudi, china and the likes and you do not understand their norms and culture. More so you lack the idea of how to pay for good and services over there. So when you landed at the country airport and the driver noticed you didn't understand their language the driver might decide to charge you more and dupe you because of lack of understanding their cultures and language so it is very important to understand and have a basic knowledge which is a foundation of anything you want to do or else you can be a loser and get broke at any given time. More so many people come with amazing offers through their advertising such as ads, catchy images, amazing sites that are well designed that says make $50,000 in just two weeks many people will think is very simple and easy to accomplish not knowing it requires a lot of time and effort for that to manifest. It takes more time and efforts to build business and internet marketing is a great way to scale up faster but wealth will not come in your first day it will definitely come through consistency the reason why ponzi scheme dupe a lot of people is that they do come with a lot of sweet offers that you won't want to let it go such as double your income in just 15 minutes not knowing is a scam but the problem most people have is that they want miracle to happen overnight they are not ready to build business that will take time to grow but they want fast money and anybody that is always a fan of fast money his or her chance of getting scammed on line is certain.

Mistakes most people make

The reason why most business failed today is because of some mistakes they make when selecting their business choice the reason is that they want to do whatever other people are doing and they won't think about the risk and the factors attached to it this is how most business owner think Mr A is into fashion business and he is successful this guarantee my success too, Mrs B is into cosmetics and beauty business line and she make good returns on her investment i will definitely succeed too but not knowing Mr A and Mrs B has done their research and homework before building their business empires they do not the years, energy, capitals, experiences these people question already had about their business before they start reaping the fruits of their labours.

This is what failed many businesses because they thought entrepreneurship is easy and they want to be addressed as a boss but in reality it stuck it is not as easy as we do look at it. Researchers have come with a conclusion that 90% of business will fail that it is only 10% business that will succeed that is to tell you entrepreneurship is a game of guts and war because your competitors are coming up with new strategies everyday that will hinder your progress in your business and send you out government policies at times can affect your business and the factor is called PESTLE Analysis which are

Political factors

Economical factors

Social factors
Technological factors
Legal factors
Ecological factor
All this analysis is to let you know you must have a strong reason before you start your business or else your Business might fail.
Internet marketing is broad
Internet marketing is a wide field but most new internet marketers get it wrong from this angle because they do not understand how to go about the journey so they have to understand the area they want to focus on may be it is content creating, website design, affiliate marketing, advertisement agency and much more they have to choose one of the mentioned above area and focus on it master it very well and specialize on it and dominate the space. Because being an expert requires area of specialization i.e. A student will not decide he wants to become a lawyer, teacher, engineer or a doctor and then chooses to attend classes randomly. No it doesn't work that way and this is how most new internet marketers begin to have problems in their journey because they decided to learn and master all the fields in marketing at a goal. They read a little here, move to the other side to partake in it training and much more even though they gather different types of skills randomly but they are not working on a good foundation because knowledge can cause problems in the long run. So it is advisable to have an area of specialization in this internet marketing field.
 It is very important and must not be taken for granted because if you can get it right from this angle then your

journey to success won't take you much time to accomplish your goal.

Creating a hot in demand product

This is another area many Internet Marketers make a huge mistake they will go ahead and import or produce a product and get a hosting and domain name, write sales letters and start sending traffic through pay advertisement for prospect to start buying this way you might end up not having any sales and you have wasted your money, energy and time putting everything together.

This is how i do mine because am one of the smartest internet marketers to live on earth am not being proud but the fact must be stated clearly here is my own logic am not a fan of any business or any industry but i am a friend of the market my philosophy is different how other digital marketers or entrepreneur reason because most of them believe so far Mr A is doing this and succeeding i will do it and succeed not knowing the market and starving crowd is what matters.

I do go out and do my research about what people want the most and they are lacking and they are ready to pay any amount for it that is how i do know the market or niche to focus on i ask question a lot more so I let my prospect do the 90% of the talking just for me to get better understanding of what they need and the remaining 10% will be a solution from then. I seal the deal because if you are the one doing all the talking you might end up losing deal they might think you are too desperate and you are in need of their money and you do not have a solution to provide for them.

No Best way to make money

Many new internet marketers easily fall for hype by big names in the industry i.e. because most successful internet marketers come up with highly converting sales letter some maybe this is your last chance to succeed online or this is one time life changing opportunity miss it or have yourself to be blame and much more if new internet marketers see this they won't have choice than to quickly add to cart or make purchase of the material not knowing there is always a way out and they will always be more opportunity to make money online because information is always coming out everyday regarding being successful online. So do not fall for all these sweet words again reason and make a choice yourself do not make a decision while on duress because you can make a decision that might later affect you in the long run. and am not saying if you see a golden opportunity that you should not go for it because opportunity has the potential to elevate you a business so far you are making the right decision.

More so do not get me wrong some of these products are very good and can be of help to your success online but what am trying to tell you is that there is always a choice and alternatives.

There is no exact formula for success

There are many ways you can succeed legitimately online. But what matters most is to love what you are doing and keep exploring and developing your Internet skills on every daily basis. Some people have been successful through content creations, affiliate marketing programs, web designing, book publishing and so on so my advice for you to focus on any of these niche and be unique. Let your approach and strategy be different from your competitors then be rest assured of success in a short or long run like I do say consistency is the key. But the only problem new internet marketers are having is that if they try something 1 to 3 times if it doesn't work they will leave it which is very wrong you are new build relationship first because without a good relationship no how you can be successful online that ids the fact.

Develop a positive mindset

There is a saying that says a positive mindset is the key that separates the best from the rest. A lot of successful Internet marketers are always confidence and let go of fear because their positive mindset is what makes them begin to achieve success online because if you are not positive and you never believe in your ability no how you can achieve success online but if you are yet to make your first money online you will never believe internet marketing works this same internet marketing has make some smart marketers millions of dollar in the past and still bring them a lot of money presently. You can begin to start making money through sponsor ads on your site through facebook ads or google adsense because once you start making money online you will be unable to sleep again because new ideas will start coming to your mind everyday and you won't hesitate to implement it that is the power of internet marketing.

Freedom and security

This is one of the most essential things you need to put into consideration which is freedom and security because when you start an internet marketing business without proper planning your relations may think or feel you are compromising their financial security state because security may be directly related to your mindset and it is very important and most essential to consider it in more explanation and well detailed as not having the proper motive and mindset because if this is not put into consideration properly it can deprive you from moving forward and achieving the success you are rightfully and legally entitled to what am trying to explain is about finance security state which requires positive mindset and it is all about you perceiving security state from your own unique initiative.

It is indeed subjective because there is no acceptable standard on what financial security is all about. Some people view the term security as a field and an area of specialization. While some people refer to it as having a monthly income that is beyond their living expenditures and no debts or having savings that is approximately to a month or 3 to 5 years annual salary. It can also be anything different from one person to another because most of us have been raised with the perspective that you have to work very hard and diligently to achieve good grades and later find a steady reliable job that pay us a stable monthly salary why some of us have been brought up to avoid owing people at all cost and some of us are brought up to save few out of our monthly salary this is to tell you we were brought up from different background and our ways of life will definitely be different from each other and the term change is perceived to affect or threaten our financial security and it may cause complications for many people. In a nutshell you must consider security

and reason about it from a totally different angle or area. It is very important why the word freedom is a direct opposite of security because the more you are secured the lesser freedom you gain. Freedom can come in any form of way but the freedom most people prefer today is financial freedom that is anytime they are in need of money they should have a source that provides money for them easily without any disturbance so that is my take on freedom and security.
Having a negative sense of security
Many people did not believe in security and they need to change their perspective of reasoning about security because it is important to have trust and believe in it you have to remember that freedom such as working from home will definitely decrease financial security and it doesn't mean you can't have a rise in income. Have you ever put this into consideration that working at home may actually be safer and good beyond working for a business owner beside you will not only have more freedom but they will never be a superior or a boss that will sack you more so you can really begin to earn base on your abilities and efforts because most firms always make as much profit as possible while paying their workers peanut.
You have to reason about this. I am not saying you should resign or quit your job. I am just stating that you will make more money working for yourself at home than working for boss at work.
What I am trying to tell you is that your positive mindset will play a vital role in achieving your dreams and goals in life. More so some people don't have the

skills or ability to work from home and that is why they work for a company or a boss.

For you to be a successful entrepreneur it will require a lot of hard work and a positive mindset because entrepreneurship is very hard. What I am just trying to say is that there are many opportunities for Internet marketers to be wealthy more than someone working for a boss but it requires some time to get there but it really worth the time so far you know what you are doing.

Scarcity and abundance

These two terms are near to freedom and security and they are both focus on mindset more so people that know the worth of perceived job security above financial freedom they also take good job into consideration and money by implicating which can lead to scarcity. Scarcity is a principle that can make you make more money with easy because people can pay you any amount so far you have a value to offer which solve their problems and abundance here is making more money and benefit through the term scarcity because once a product is hot in demands and fewer people only have it those few can decide to sell it multiply by two or three of the real price that is the power of scarcity and the abundance is more in returns.

You need to be applying scarcity principle at times in your business for you to create that urgency in the prospect for them to make a purchase because most consumers love postponement but if they hear only 1 bottle left or slot left they will be eager to quickly make a purchase and this increases the conversion rate.

Reason and think by yourself'
This is also very important because many people don't
have the ability to reason themselves and they can't see
opportunity themselves. They prefer someone else to
always think on their behalf this does happen because
they do not believe in their own ability which is very
bad and can deprive their progress in the long run. I
urge new internet marketers to be the type that make
research on their own and they should always believe
in their ability because if you are used to meeting
people to think for you they might later give you an
advice or strategy that may not go in line with your
business or field of study because they are not the one
in the business but they will just give you some advice
based on their own experience and philosophy the only
way to get started is to believe in your own ability and
have a positive mindset that you can achieve your goals
and dream without someone else reasoning for you
because your success and failure lies in your hand not
in their own hands.
Is money the root of all evil?
This question is so straight forward and almost
everybody on the surface of this earth knows money as
the causes of evil because money is so powerful it can
make you do and undo. As we all know that money is
anything that is generally acceptable as a medium of
exchange and as for payment of debt.
Money also turns some people to semi god people
worship them just because of the money they have, it
can make the rich oppress the poor.
Sometime ago many people that lead an organisation
have the belief that money is the cause and root of all

evil that nobody can avoid it but one should not fully concentrate on it, and also certainly not be chased then some people have the believe that can it be a coincidence that most of these people doesn't have much money to live on or what is your own take on money more so some people can say it openly they like money and can't toy with it more so many people are raised to get a lucrative job and make more money to support their family but you should not have the love of too much money at heart. Or what is your take on this more so can loving money become a problem. Let assume you are not comfortable with the idea of loving money. What is your feeling for pets like cats or dogs? Is there anything wrong to say you love your pet or love your work and I know it is obvious you will say there is nothing wrong in loving your pets and such is applicable to monetary aspects too.

Have a second thought about it. What i just see and observe so far is that people takes on loving money are very different from each other because some people will say having the love of money at at is good why others will say having the love is not good because money is the root of all evil and to be frank with you if you ask these two set of people about the saying they will have points to back their words. There is a saying that says many people will suffer because of money, others will die because of money, Nothing can be done without money, everything is done by money and lastly money is the evil of the world.

But on the other hands the important and the characteristic of money is very essential such as Durability

Divisibility
Portability
Acceptability
And much more this is to tell you money is very
important in all mankind lives and it also cause
problem in mankind lives so it is vice versa
Risk and return
Risk is a game of guts and it is not for the weaken but
the brave that is to tell you that is not a must you
should take a very big or huge risk if you want a huge
returns in an investment this is to tell you small risk at
times can make you rich for the rest of your life and
why big risk at time can cause you loss and damages it
is all about the ability of seeing possibilities and
believing in the dream before striking the deal. There
are a lot of investors today such as Bill Gates, Warren
Buffet and the likes they built up a good reputation and
expertise investment. Most especially warren buffett he
has really made a lot of billions of dollars on the stock
exchange market today why other investors have lost
their investment that is to tell you risk can be profitable
and can as well result as loss. So it is advisable to have a
better understanding of how things work before
investing in it or else it will end up becoming a gamble
because you do not know what you are investing on
you just decide to risk your money on something you
don't know how it works.
 More so many people perceive internet marketing as a
gambling you won't be surprised if run a sponsor ad
you will see many people writing on your ad that you
should help them that they need money very fast and
my candid advice for these set of people is to get a job

that pays daily, weekly or monthly because they don't know internet marketing is not a get rich quick business it requires a lot of time sacrifice and efforts before it later pays.

You need to be consistent and hardworking to make good money online in your business as we all know that Rome wasn't built in a day and road to success always comes with complications and a lot of challenges prayer and dedication is the only way to achieve an end result and goal.

Believe in your ability

I do say a positive mindset is the key that separates the best from the rest some people will say they are desperate that they want success but their mind is full of impossibility and poverty and there's no way you can be successful without a positive mindset that is the fact. You have to believe in yourself that should be your fixed asset that is anything is possible. You must represent possibilities and you must try to learn from two people.

People that have done your exact business in the past but they fail and the second set of people are people that are doing it presently and they have succeeded these are two ideas you need for you to be successful in your journey. More so you must believe in what you are doing despite any challenges you might be facing and you must also be confident enough on your work for others to believe in you.

Before you start selling a product try as much as possible to learn about it properly and problem it solves before you start selling because you must believe in your product and service because anything aside is will be considered to be fraud and scam. And also have this in mind the more you do something the more you will be good at it. Practise makes you perfect.

You must be specific

You should have this in mind that you are not meant to serve everybody you must have an area of specialization because if you want to do many things at a goal it will cause you losing out and not achieving your goals all you need is to focus on a niche examples fashion, beauty, logistic, agriculture, transportation and the likes you have to choose one niche and understand how your niche works and operate from A to Z because this is the only way you can dominate your niche than to be running up and down.

And this the only way you will be respected and recognised in your niche

You will also be in a position to figure out your prospect and they will believe in you and feel you understand what their problems really look like this is achievable through focusing on your niche and you must have the ability to craft a sales letter that really communicate with your audience more so they must feel that your sales letter is written because of them with this your customer will pay for your service and product just because they believe you are doing them a great benefit.

Online marketing and offline marketing

A new internet marketer must understand the similarities and differences between online and offline marketing. I have been in online marketing for 5 years and i must confess it is very easy to sell online than offline and that is 100% truth because everything is base on trust and credibility because many people ask themselves question like where do you buy your products, why do you buy from them these are question they ask if they can say good about your service that is how referral come in without spending a dime on advertisement and you start to make more money but you must have a good reputation because credibility goes a long way and it matters a lot your customers are often not close to you but you just have to build that trust and this will happen through your dedication and good value you offer to them because if you do not offer value they will not buy from you again next time.

That is the reason online market is profitable and far better than offline marketing.

Building a relationship and Trust online

Relationship and trust is very essential because without working on it you can't be successful online you must know how to convince potential prospects that already have a business relationship with you because it is their best interest to contact you and it is because you understand their desire or needs and you can provide them solutions to their problems.

You must be a problem solver that is the only way people will listen to you.

To be realistic and be candid It is very difficult to build a commercial relationship online because you can't compare friends that are close to each other to the relationship between your local grocery seller the imagine is very big more so there is always a relationship chances they are various way to build relationship online such as prompt customer response, good product encouraging words, follow up, bonuses, prompt delivery and much more these are some strategies to apply to build relationship online and scale up your business and with all these strategies you will always be registered in their mind and they will always contact you for their future needs and also introduce you and your business to their relations. When you run a sponsor ad to your website. Ensure you make your ads very appealing, easily to under, a call to action and so on. The key here is to make it simple. Because people are always scared and bored of reading too much online.

Online services and selling needs a suitable approach This aspect of internet marketing needs a very logical approach because most people dislike landing up on a website that consists of too many banners and ads more so you need to be logical and very illustrative not to scare customers away from your website. Let them know you can solve their problem and that is the reason they land on your website.

Provide useful information and tips to solve their problems and let them know you have the right solution to solve their problems.

You must have this at the back of your mind that customers are always right because they want to spend their money on your service.

Even though they are at fault you don't need to fight we them you have to say good and appealing words to them because an angry customer today can be the best customer tomorrow not only that you can gain a lot of customers through the customer that is a business lesson most internet marketer are not taking into consideration.

If you would love to build a successful online business you must develop a good reputation and build trust by providing great customer services to your prospects. Make use of good customer service as a marketing tool and ensure you let it be your advantage and opportunity of turning a problem into a good and positive experience for a customer and also know that you will not only keep the clients but also derive a valuable merit for your business and this can skyrocket your profit overnight.

Goal settings

The term goal setting is all about having clear objectives and having a plan on working towards achievement of the goal.

Goal setting or aim gives you an opportunity to visualize that the future will be bright. Apj Abdul Kalam of blessed memory says Dream is not what you see in your sleep but it is the thing that doesn't make you sleep. It is just like a goal setting if you are clear about it you will not rest until you achieve it.

Goal will always come true and can be achievable through effective planning because without proper planning on how you want to go about it or achieve it you may not end up achieving the said goals.

That is the reason the 4 key elements of planning are very important towards achieving a goal which is the end result.

A goal can be planning to start up a business, A goal can be planning to buy a car, A goal can be planning to buy properties and much more but without 4 key elements of planning it will be meaningless.

The 4 key element of planning are as follow

1. Objective
2. Action
3. Implementation
4. Resources

Objective means the goal you have, the dream you have, the thought you have, a project you are yet to implement but it is in your mind and it is giving you sleepless night.

Action is the follow up the necessary steps that you will need and take towards achieving the said goal it maybe through seeking advice from expert in a field, it maybe through savings, or financial institution assistant and so on that is action

Implementation is putting your goals and plan together it maybe through organising a seminar or educating people about your goal what you stand to achieve with your goals that is implementation

Resources this is the capital needed, labour need, asset needed to implement your plans for you to achieve your end result which is your goal.

With all these explanations so far I believe by now you will get a better understanding of goal setting and I will urge you to implement it in your business for it to elevate you in all your endeavours.

Be big in thinking and be realistic

You must always be big in thinking and reasoning. Do not go for the small but go for the big but you must be realistic through your thinking and how to achieve it.

For example you earn $1,500 dollar per month you can set a goal of earning $5,000 per month which can be achievable through proper planning and working towards achieving because anything is possible more so anything the mind can think is achievable. Also move with people that always have a high goal and they do achieve learn the legitimate strategy they use in implementing their plan and how they do achieve it. We need to keep learning everyday because technology is out to make life easier. analog days are gone we are in a digital age now and life has been so easy just believe in yourself and see possibilities in what you do that is when you will know anything is achievable.

Having a business plan

Once you have stated your goals the next step is to sketch or diagram your business plan out. This is going to be time consuming but it is the number one way to get started. By sticking to this principle you will definitely have a business of your dream in reality in some hours time most firms spend a lot of money on business plan because they believe it is very essential besides they recruit consultants and make a lot of research because they want success. You are so lucky you will not be needing all these just follow my guide then you are good to go more so when you have a good business plan you will be confident to succeed, make more money online and you will never think of failure for once. These are the merit towards having a clearly define business plan

Establishing people demands

It is very important to know exactly what people needs and they are desperate to buy it at any cost beside having the best product will never pay your bills if there is no demand for it you must considering making use of search engine to know what people are looking for because search engine ranks website based on relevancy and the right keywords.

Because then the only way to make money online is to discover what people demands look like and as a smart internet marketer yours is to make it available for them and start smiling to your bank account.

I recommend you should start making use of Google keyword tools Such as Google trend, Google ad word and the like because you need to find out if there is a demand in your niche because your only work as an internet marketer is to solve problems.

Problem solving

A solution provider to any problem is the only person that has financial freedom because you will always make money and you will never be broke for once. Try and always look for people's demand and always position yourself and sell to people that are in need of your service that is what smart internet marketer does.

Because many people are always searching for solutions to specific problems and these sets of people are easier to convert to potential customers than people just browsing on the internet and found your product coincidentally so the difference is clear. Once you have researched the problem in your niche and you have the solution to it.

Then you are good to go.

Promoting through affiliate marketing

Now that you have found a niche or a market that shows there is a desperate need and demand for your service and they are a lot of competitors in the market space the next thing you must put into consideration is to look for an affiliate program platform that you can put your product on and promote it easily for a good returns we have many of affiliate network niche such as jvzoo, warrior plus, clickbank, infusionsoft and the likes all these platform will scale you up very easily because they are a lot of people who already to promote for you on certain commission on each sales you get through their affiliate links. Because if there are no competitions in your niche that means you are not in a market that consists of hungry buyers that need a solution more so your end result is to sell to customers and make your money after delivery of the product to the prospect.

You must have a plan for your business

Having a better plan for one business is very good and it will have effects in the long run because there is a word that says he who fails to plan definitely plans to fail.

This is why manpower planning is very important for any company aspiring for success or an already successful company because manpower planning is all about envisioning and planning on how to move the company from it current manpower position to a higher level so it is important to get it right and also consider establishing departments for your company for prompt and good services to your customers.

This will make me go to Human resources management department which consist of the following

Recruitment management department

Employee management department

Attendance management department
Shift management department
Level management department
Payroll management department
The six departments under the human resources
management department listed below are very
important and will help each department to
understand their works. It will also be of help to the
management level in the company from the Top level
management to the lowest level management.
Customers is always right
The word customer is always right is very common in
the business world and that is 100% naked truth. You
must always be doing things or providing value that
will favour your customers even though when the
customer did the wrong thing still be calm let the
customer know in his or her conscience that they are
the one guilty or at fault with this simple principle you
can dominate your niche put customers first before
anything let them feel so special even like a king or a
president of a country with this kind of humility act you
will stand out and be respected in your business
because you already built a good relationship and
reputation around your business
Don't be too eager for the money at first but what
matters the most is a good customer relation once you
can stick to this you will make more money than being
anxious for money i.e. solve the problem properly then
success is yours.

Conclusion

I strongly believe and hope the information in this book
will be of help to anybody aspiring to be an internet

marketer because the lesson in this book are well researched and properly written to the best of my knowledge

My goal and happiness in this planet world is to eradicate illiteracy in my own little way and add value to people's life because if i give you money it will definitely finish but if i teach you a lesson it will never finish it can be useful to you for the rest of your life. This book is meant to serve as a guide for aspiring or new internet marketers. I wish you success in all your works in life.

THE END   THE END   THE END